Interludes To The Indian Buddha

Gaurav Krishnan

BookLeaf Publishing
India | USA | UK

Presentation by *BookLeaf Publishing*

Web: www.bookleafpub.com

E-mail: info@bookleafpub.com

ISBN: 9789358369861

First edition 2023

DEDICATION

To my my mother Shanti Gopalakrishnan, my
father Gopalakrishnan Raman, and my sister
Swati Gopalakrishnan

And also my dear late grandmother Smt. Kamala
Sankaranarayanan (1943-2023)

ACKNOWLEDGEMENT

This book is my second effort writing poetry. I have come a long way in my life's journey and I couldn't do it without the support of my family and close friends.

These verses are a slight detour from my first book The Indian Night, but remain true to my experiences although they're written in a slightly different style, following my influences of reading and listening to the beat poets of the 1950s and '60s. As is the case with beat poetry, it hits home better when heard, in spoken word, just like several old recordings of poets like Jack Kerouac and Charles Bukowski, which served as the inspiration and blueprint for this book.

You could perhaps even play some of the music I've made as a musician and artist (Ghost Intent) while reading these poems and they're my spin on beat poetry of the 21st century electronic music generation (as the book's cover page suggests). It was jazz that propagated the beat generation back then, and it's the music we now make on computers that has prompted a shift and seen music expand and evolve into several new genres, and who knows what genres will come about in the future.

But these poems are very much meant for music and are a bit musical, and I might just record audio clips of them at some stage. I've tried writing them in a new style, writing longer poems that tell stories, so this was a bit of an experiment, but I hope you dig these verses.

For whoever you are, wherever you may be, when you read these verses and these themes, I hope you resonate with the moments, emotions, ideas and narratives encompassed in this book.
These verses, intentionally left open to interpretation, have been written to encourage you to think and feel; a collection of words to come back to that aim to help you find the value of art, chase peace instead of happiness since peace is much more sustainable for longer periods.

These verses encourage living in more serenity, to lead a mindful life, and, to celebrate the beauty of art and of course, the glorious interludes. If my words achieve this, then my role as a writer, musician and poet is fulfilled.
Thank you for purchasing my book,
Gaurav

PREFACE

-A few quotes I penned down on social media that I felt would set the precedent for this book-
"It was as though the sea spoke to me & carried the weight on my shoulders into its vast expanse. As though, the tides decided that I was to be forgiven & restored to a true empty state, of solitude, and peace within, where I could feel the fire from the sun burning into my very being. As though, the sky knew that staring into the horizon was exactly what I needed for solace. Here I was, by the sea, & the healing & tranquility it brought me. Another day that I was free. Another day to celebrate & contemplate my place in the world & how far I had come on my journey. The intricate nuances of nature & simple things merged with my desire to be totally immersed in the moment went hand in hand with the urgency, steadiness & coolness of a bird's flight. Where the sky & its contours revealed streams of light through the clouds, & despite having no groundbreaking discoveries, I was happy: The word I dread, because its nature is so fleeting, but maybe something more sustainable in peace. Peace carries you through despite the blues that seep in unannounced & unplanned, like a telemarketing salesman's

phone call at lunchtime. I see in nature similarities to music, it's a grand cosmic gig, a glorious band, playing jazz, blues & rock shifting in colour & texture & hue depending on nature's mood. And us, well, we're the ardent concertgoers taking the experience in. We must put on our concert shoes, and revel the days & nights away because we have no other choice but to rejoice. And in what we give back to the world, we are the instruments making the music. And In the end, when we're on the way out, when this grand show is coming to a close, there will be wild applause from the fervent crowd for the music that you made....."
 - Gaurav Krishnan

"The Blues. You can't write about what the Blues are in the pages or annals of a book. Nor can you put it in words when you talk to people. You don't see it in shiny, happy, and gleaming faces at parties or pubs or on the faces of every passerby when you're walking down the street. You see it in their eyes; their sad eyes. It's a feeling. It's an emotion. It's an expression. It's life talking; life taking the piss. It's life telling you this is Earth & down here you've got to balance it all out. Good & bad. Life ain't all sunshine, clear skies & roses. Life can bring you down. Life can hurt. Life can destroy. Life doesn't give a fuck about your feelings. That's why we sing. You don't sing because you're happy & you're fine & when everything is going well. You sing because you've got the Blues" - Gaurav Krishnan

This book was conceived to offer a bit of solace & to urge reflection. It's meant for readers who dare to be more. The people who battle their silent struggles but still show up, do the best they can and persevere. The people who go on despite the blues. Poetry is my current way of leaving something   timeless behind; my perspective through my art, which has coincided with the music I've released as a producer under my artist moniker Ghost Intent.

If you're picking up this book and giving the poems in it a read, I hope it leaves a lasting impression on you and urges you to think, act, and do beyond the conventions of society and everyday life. I hope this inspires you to venture into creating your own art, to explore, to live life to the fullest, and to keep pushing yourself to be more and do more despite how hard it can get at times.

I hope these words filter down and make for a smooth and cool read, for the "interludes" of this experience, this consciousness, we call life. These poems are for a bit of respite from the frantic rush of life & are little anecdotes and remnants to keep you trudging on consistently and bravely in your quest for whatever you want to achieve out of life.

My grandfather the late P.A. Raman once wrote a piece in the 1930s after he moved to Bombay to work as a journalist titled, "Be Bold, Be Resolute".

All these years on, my grandfather's words remain. Unfortunately, my father can't find that published article which was one of my grandad's most insightful pieces from his youth. But my message to you today as you read this book is, no matter what happens in life remember to "Be bold, be resolute"
And quite importantly to also make room for art in your life; art of any kind. Lastly, remember to sing & dance to the music in those brief pauses, and take in and celebrate the mellow interludes in your life....

Imprints

Of enlightenment
& knowledge: acquired, shared
       & handed down

a story,
a perspective
       that each soul has in its intricate
design
       The lush wave
       that flows in
       w/ thoughts
       that must be lightly let go,
       w/ a breath
the fireworks
comets; land, skies, and sea
that make up the 70mm IMAX experience
lay bare the moment —spinning sounds—
       life lived at the interjunction
       of a new millennium

       We must latch swiftly
to the pale present
to be breathed
to be held, adorned
       come from wide & far

                        & grace these holy lands

              Drift down the Ganges,
              the Jari mountain side,
              A train ride to Suratgarh
              & a foggy journey from Bikaner

A cliff drive in Gwalior,
The winds of Bokaro
The Gokarna coastline embedded in Om
the rainy deluge of camaraderie
                              in the city of
Mumbai,
                  the unerring & mesmeric calm
of Odayam,
                  the dancing lights & a campfire
in Kodaikanal

              it's here —the abode—
              the experience
Imprints

Freedom: Is it?

Freedom lies in
a full English breakfast
& that first cigarette
staring into a sky
that begins its daily rise, rinse
      & calm
fluctuations; calculated change
       that mixes with the
first song
       of the day that you
play
headphones or bluetooth speakers
the ones you bought online

clouds shapeshifting,
like a thought bubble
     & a machinist's
amphitheater
     like clockwork
     from goblins to
Henkelpotts
that pirate with his binoculars
that expansive buffet
that animal
or face in the sky

                        you've seen it somewhere
                        now it's up there
                        it's staring down at you
                        (peripheries)
but you know it's a cloud

Freedom across the horizon
                                —sun
kingdom—the usual dream
                                of going
somewhere
                                or wanting a new
beginning
                                a fresh start
new country
new culture
that pizzazz
French food
until you get there
& stay around a while
maybe find some friends,
a lover
get tired
& then you want to come back

Freedom of hearts beating
                                To reach out and
grab the beat

                                 to feel it, touch it,
opaqueness
                                 rhythm of a blood
moon
                                           &
drift-dazes away
                                     as it
flees
 —a dance —of what it means
to be living
this consciousness
this human
body & experience
                        not alone:
                              but alone with
everybody
in motion
that shimmers, nuanced
                          & immersive like an
electric impasse

In this moment: do as you please,
                   free to think, do, live
                   like an elaborate progressive
rock song
                   (in production)
                   the studio engineer is late
                   the coffee is getting cold
                   the session band is warming up

to play a new guitar lick
& forget it
to scribble some words
or to explore
    a daydream
    & to fall into the ruckus & cycles
    of neurons flaring
(they have their way, at times)
    but must flow and be freed

—a gust of wind — the incoming sea breeze
     Marine Drive
     rainfall - while sipping chai
     a dash of ginger
     at a small tapri
Who are you people I'm sharing this tapri with?
What is your story?
"And then the market crashed & my put hit its
stop-loss"
"My kiraya ka paisa didn't come in time"
"I'm leaving for my village tomorrow"
"Urgent meeting....."—ashed my cigarette— and
left

a tune that played on the net radio
or you heard in a passing car
or one that's stuck in your head
       at an odd time:
almost out of nowhere

                                        and you just
sing it in your head
                                        as if you're a
musician
                                        (everyday
artists)

an idea that might be worth
it's weight in gold or suck

a kick of a football
7 v 7 on the turf nearby
you're having a good game
                        nice first touches &
turns
                        scored and assisted a
few
                        but you can't play
the whole 90
—drinks break — your lungs are old
& your stamina
has been receding
like your hairline

the start of the weekend fixture
that you've be waiting for
                        —the kit is worn—
crowds moving into the stadium

                              w/ their excited
children
                              sifting & filling up the
spaces
                              scarves, colors,
smiles, emotions
except you're in another country
behind a TV screen &
yelling into the void
when your team scores

a sprint from a runner
trying to get fit
                    or to finish the 100 meter race
                    at Priyadarshini park

a loud laugh
at a podcast joke
or at some shit you saw on the feed
                              —all comedians are
innately sad—

the anticipation just at the beginning of a film
before the opening scene
                              the excitement of what
it could bring
                              as you take your seat
w/ the expensive caramel popcorn

                              (the opening credits
begin)

a new discovery — in the ruins of Indonesia
                    a documentary of animals in
the Arctic,
            the group of women that just entered
the bar
            and you don't know which one to hit on,
so you just take a sip

a tribute to a Blues musician
 —ramblin' blues — a black sharecropper who
lived and died
                        playing his six string
                        & howlin' at the moon
                        (moans & groans)
 life in the early 20th century
                to be free
                but he's now embedded on vinyl
you can see the glint in his eye
& feel his melody
                not so much a fingerstyle master
but something raw in his voice
                same 4 beat bars
        same old crossroads sound

—a bassline change— at a techno gig
& you're really feeling it,

until you see those dudes
going berserk in the first row
the front; facing the DJ
& near the speakers
                        that chick in front of you
                        who looks like some kind
                        of medieval goddess in the
dark
                        sipping her drink &
swinging
                        w/ her perfect hair &
moving
                        like a black swan in a 21st
century ballet
& you're enchanted for a while
then the crowd singalong track comes along
& they play a pop song you hate
& you see her singing it word for word
with the emotion of all her exes
that dumped her put together
so know that it's your cue to leave

—pinging— the internet router getting fixed
after hours of no connectivity
you don't know what you've got
till it's gone
but everybody panics when
the net goes out

a passionate kiss from a lover
after returning from travel related work
                        you haven't seen each other
face to face
                        in months, seasons,
                        except for video calls
she cooks your favorite meal
lights up the bedroom with candles
puts on CSNY
                    the sex is wild after
                    (evanescent orgasms)

the hope that the new haircut looks good
just as the barber is halfway through
                        thinking "please, please, don't
fuck this up"
                        but then coming to terms
                        w/ the way you look
after the hairdresser is done
& convincing yourself it looks fine
from the moment you leave the parlor
up until two weeks after

a philosopher's words & essays
making sense
even in the 2020s
                        logic, thought — reason—
                        from a forgotten time
suddenly it makes sense

and you take what you can
maybe even write about it
                    who knows?
              someone could read what you wrote
              3 centuries into the future &
              the cycle could repeat

the walk on freshly changed pavement
just around the street you live
but now there are
lights on the street for a festival
sweets and savories
colours, crowds & marching bands

bedtime stories
summer after winter

                              come hell or go high

freedom is here

Fading City

People just hover
& fade away
As you pass them by
Along the way

Fluctuations
ripples that bend thru
the ether, the atmosphere
memories
(momentary)
(momentum picking up)
the system is booting
90s PC

countdown on a clock
to a satellite launch
somewhere, mysterious
all sails to another land
a land unknown
a land you've hoped for
any land, just somewhere else
but you pray it's paradise

hope dangles
w/ rhythm
a drive
w/ a shifting scenery
hillsides
plains, no roadways there
when you look out of the window
a man there at the train junction
he's the only one for miles

but the road to
El Puerto de Santa María
& a shipyard
in Medellín
& the landing strip
in a Carribean island you
just discovered
like starting a voyage

the streets are empty
the town brings you down
& fades away
As you walk along

a soldier salutes
like the beckoning of destiny
which changes with choice

a cocaine rush
a soul cigarette
& midnight music

It's bitter
it's incomplete
like a letter undelivered
& change runs its course
& fades away
just like the song
you wrote today

this distance
a collection of strewn
collages
An hour when the sun
Dives into the unknown
& the vastness of
The expanse
that sinks into
The frontier, the cut b/w
sea and sky
that divide

When we floated
on rafts
& rode the river

grade IV rapids
under a holy bridge

& smiled fondly
At the music
& the moments

Life moves like a locomotive
but moments move like
slow traffic
there's time to take it all in
& not complain

only to find
a fire
a home
an ocean

this horizon

this fading city

Bombay Summer

Bombay summer
—the city is silent—
the metal isn't dragging
the college kids
aren't filing through the street

this morning of no alarms
something about today:
a day
to draw & paint again
on this canvas
of time
of mellow stillness

A day of happiness
fleeting,
but not today
a longer lingering
of peace

Quiet sounds
& big calm
Birds floating,
adorning the contours
of the cloudy sky

making their way
to my balcony view

Amongst the trees
that are alive
& garage roofs
                morning smoke
                coffee & pancakes
                & window
of opportunity

A book & pen
of ink that flows
thru my brain
                in words aplenty
& morning brew

Words on a laptop
piano chromatic
the gift of the present
& blue

The music of gentle
                vibrations & tranquil
                like the score
                to the soundtrack
of a peace piece

—a montage —

        of shots
        that echo
        mindful being

A new dawn
a soft interplay of colours
As the sunlight
touches my skin

        Another day free
& glorious

        of peace around
        & peace inside
        within this scene
        and life's gig

    that's without a rehearsal
(brightside)

Aha Revolution

Of the natural course
& guerilla warfare
                    Unhinged Babylon
                    The rocky road
                    to Dublin
& the passageways
to El Dorado

Zapata's radio
(interference)
                Guevara's cigar
                (smoke & mirrors)
                            & Cortez's guitar
                            (water dance)

A mix
& transitions:
                we're in this cellular
                provocation
                & awakening

To light the flames
of adventure
of exploration
                an act of faith
& to explore we must:

                        free and uninfected
                        as the seas & skies
                        nod in cohesion
                        of a celestial gig

w/ brass sections

in cloud symphonies
& old mobile ringtones
                        a poor home
                        unfed & a small bed

drawing the curtains
open:
                        to the next act
                        the next moment
where the mind
is immersed
in no idea
greater than
            existence
            & freedom

the fight & duty
of pistoleros
of an Indian sun
                who did not dwell
on empty stomachs
                or heartbreak
Aha revolution

Blood In The Wind

A rugged field
The poppies grow
for lives unlived
the good that
died young
in arms
to the end

The blood rushes
thru the wind
down the drain
w/ dancing clouds
stories
& a words of change
—a storm—
that could approach

Bellowing wind
that blows
against the clothes line

See through
inside
w/ open eyes
scar & bone

a battle
a soldier
a survivor

of a thousand raging
psychic wars

Seven Shamans

Ultra supersonic
Another tale
of a distant sun
The river
that runs w/ the flow:

        from a glacier
        to refuse no seas
        merging
        & stirring
        into the vastness

 to return to ice again

No more disguise
uncovered
in spiritual design:
        stillness
& a potent potion

Seven shamans
call from afar:
      in visions
      in ambient galaxies
      in astral projections
      in vivid parting
of the sandstorm

      & in waves that
      change their force
      in walks between
parallel worlds

they tell their stories:
     in taxi halts
     & signs
     in playgrounds
     in fields
     in advertisement hoardings
   & that dream
   that was cast upon
   your consciousness

A collection of dots
on maps that
     lead to the pirate loot
     the golden war chests
     the old sailor's drinking money
     the forgotten worker's
     food wages
arrows & compasses
forest mercenaries
—& the resistance—

dimly lit lamps, flaming
the lanterns of bright
     & spirit vine

to spend moments
on the rituals

Ever here
ever now

Man With A Movie Camera

Montage begins:
shots of that woman
the way she glides
& moves
her charms, her subtle
head turns & smiles
        & lights that cigarette
        against a wall
        The envy of every passerby
        sidewalk or car
that short hair & speaking eyes
        she's waiting.....

        cut to:
high shot
a group of sullen people
entering the premises for business
w/ no facade
        like ants
        scurrying
        for that last
        bit of sugar
        that 40 ounce
that stuff that
beats your wife's coffee

they enter the building.....

                        cut to:
shot of a stranded traveler
on the side of a hi-way
vehicles pass by
a shot of scale
of the surroundings
                the hitchhiker enters the
scene
                shot in the middle
                of the road
                both protagonists on either
side
it's aesthetic
a car approaches
                and comes to a halt.....

                cut to:
a room in Paris
a couple
in love
on either side
of an open balcony entrance
                he's got the champagne
                she's got the lipstick
                he's wearing a tuxedo
                her low cut black dress
                reveals just enough of skin

fireworks go off
in the sky at a distance
         The Eiffel Tower backdrop
         the shot is central
         in the room
         both on either side
as the firecrackers burst
         they take their shoes off.....

         cut to:
The camera follows the taxi
in Mumbai city
attached next to the bumper
         the wheel keeps turning
         the sun is going down
         the crowds of people
         wander on their way
night looms
the sky darkens
now the city's lights
enchant
camera pans:
         the neon sign of
         Jazz by the Bay
         on the Queen's necklace stretch
         the lights
a shot from a friend's terrace
         that overlooks Marine Drive
         the Haji Ali Juice Center

the old Crossroads mall
that meal at Noorani
the chaos of Saath Rasta
The progressing shots
of Mahalaxmi Race Course
the taxi stops at gate no.4
she was there once
after a gig
& there was something in her eyes
waiting.....

cut to:
a child playing w/ chopsticks
she's from Japan
her parents, immigrants
in the United States
she's young but she's got
something inside her
music-art-flow
she doesn't know it yet
she's tapping those
chopsticks just like
drumsticks

cut to:
shot of a stage's lights
a shot of the crowd
screaming
as the band faces

                        the girl is in her twenties
                        she's the drummer
                        she plays a few rimshots
                        & hits the cymbals
she starts the count.....

                        cut to:
her parents tell her
not to play with the chopsticks
they're old fashioned
                she stops.....

                cut to:
library period
a kid walks around
the library has
wooden flooring
& has some slightly
elevated sections
                        book cupboards
                        w/ glass openings
                        he's looking at
                        the shelves
                        & sees a book &
picks it up.....

it's Mein Kampf
he goes to the librarian
to issue the book

the librarian
an old Catholic guy
w/ a beard & glasses:
                        gives the kid a look
                        but issues it anyway
                        the kid reaches home from
school
after watching his
favourite cartoons
He goes to his room
opens the book & reads
he starts to read.....

                    cut to:
it's WWII
a man hides
in the rubble:
                he's Polish
                he's on the run
                he's hiding from the Nazis
                he finds an abandoned
                house w/ a piano
                he sits down
he begins playing
a German officer enters.....

                        cut to:
that kid is now in college
Tarantino's Inglorious has released

he downloads the Torrent file
it's over by the time he's
done with smoking some pot
in his apartment w/
his flat mates
& ordering his biryani
w/ chicken 65 on top
& nice mughlai gravy
for dinner

he begins watching.....
(A Morricone like score starts)

                      cut to:
1930s brass band
black singers & dancers
the Ritz in Atlantic City
prohibition in America:
                      the mobsters enter
                      they occupy the tables
                      champagne-cocaine
                      the broads on their laps
they're living it up
Capone, Rothstein,
Lansky, Luciano,
Nucky
"a kind word &
a gun"
                  stacks of green paper

                they just don't make them like
that anymore
                something about
                the roaring 20s & 30s
he's in an old South Indian
township in 2010
but contemplates about
how he'd have caught
a boat to New York
if he was alive
back then

                cut to:
A man now in his 30s
writing a screenplay
a bedroom studio
the same room
same street
same house
Bombay:
                but it all comes back
                all those hours
                after playing w/ friends
                & playing computer games
                glued to the TV
summer vacations
w/ back to back movies
on Star Movies & HBO
for hours together

                the dots align
                that's all he did
                as a kid after school
& the sullen nights after
playing at the pub
in college
                a laptop & a movie
w/ munchies

he begins writing.....
the ideas, the shots, the flow
seamlessly
there's art to make

From the past to the future
Man with a movie camera

La Pausa

That infinite pause
the moment
you were born

that switch of play
　　　　　　　　from one flank to the other
　　　　　　　　in the middle of a game when
the players,
　　　　　　　　the crowd and watching
world
pause along with you

the intermission:
　　　　　　　　between seeing the lightning
　　　　　　　　& hearing the thunder
　　　　　　　　when everything is suspended
in anticipation of each other

when you take
　　　　　　　　a moment to remember the
memory
to write in your diary

The pause for:

        the good days & the gigs of
tomorrow
        where she waits in the wings
for the next song

(sonic sounds)
& she puts it on tape
        & dances
like a sky symphony
        in the boundaries of your
vision
not just seen, but felt & acknowledged with each
passing tune

when she: steps into your world
      & she moves & sways
      like cotton candy clouds
      & neon horizons

I've ridden
the myriad highway
        & spoken to the night

I swam into the waves
& came back after the storm

I've climbed the landfill
& torched the endless hotels

I've reached out
& been down

w/ faded memories
of the women once there, but now gone

she walks w/ me
in the sand as another groove emerges
as I played my guitar
—a rocknrolla—
—a one man band—

a goodtime girl, a friend,
to share the calamity of the passing of time &
age
for the spinning flux of moments that ebb &
flow into a painter's canvass
to offer balance underneath a bridge of troubled
tides
w/ eyes to inspire the art & repair the damage

for the stars to align:
                    the arrival of the flight
                    the warrior's return from
battle
to stop the pain
for time to heal

the hope

of harmony
songs of old lovers
& songs of celebration bands

hoping dearly
            for serenity

waiting in
La Pausa

Miles Davis To The Head

An octave
wherein all the beauty lies
ying-yang in black & white
the hypnotic jazz ensemble
the women in the crowd
short skirts and lipstick
drink in their hand
radiant light
talking in expectation
The married men
w/ children on their shoulders
to move & groove tonight

no tables
a bit prehistoric: where
we lit fires and danced
a carnival, a gathering
a tribe

a tea pot boiling somewhere
that strange loner
in the VIP section
w/ stacks of money
buying drinks for
the cutest women around

the stooge
who sets up the lights
followed by the cameraman
who would rather
work in Hollywood
or shoot a documentary

the drummer
who discovered
his talent
at his neighbors
& wants
people to move
to the beat
he's forgotten the
count
but he plays perfectly
he's from Brazil
doesn't understand
much English
but he's got bossa nova
in his veins

the piano player
whose pain
you can hear
when he plays the keys
almost like
a drift of a memory

from his life
w/ each note he hits:
that woman who left him
his father who passed away
every time he tried to
get a real job
waiting tables
driving for food delivery
but here he is
on the Steinway
under the lights
for tonight

that middle-aged British woman
who plays the cello
she's going through a divorce
she's getting the alimony
But her husband gets the kids
so her cello will weep tonight

that upright bass player
whose fingers pump like oil;
the oil that that lucky insurance employee
found in the deserts of Texas
the instrument is as big
as a hot air balloon
but he's gonna get
the low range to bounce

the brass section
"Ah brass!"
the brass that made
that biopic movie standout
tall white guy
on the saxophone
he's got some sax licks
that can make
the toughest men cry
that black guy
on the trumpet
treats the instrument
like a mistress he never
wants to leave
they've both released
albums & have been there
& done that
but every night
is a new night
they were once
on the streets
busking for pennies
but this is the dream

there's a standstill
you can hear every
breath
every sweat drop

The stage curtains open
The beat Gen Z, that fast cool sound
That jazz
That begins

In my room
Miles Davis — to the head

Himalayan Ice

The imminent score, I tell my roommates stories
of mountain beings,
dissolved in idol worship who wear beads that
take the shape of their necks
& are wrapped around their wrists a selfish
barter of the energy trade

w/ rough skin to reflect strenuous endeavours
nose rings, piercings, sticks & carvings in stone
placed along their sacred threads around their
arms & necklines
canteens that harbour the glacial waters the
purist H2
Kanchenjunga hitchhikers of a forgotten moon

they speak a language yet to be understood by
the world
but I can hear them & understand their concerns
but today is a gift, today I celebrate 6000 ft
& perhaps a long journey of 6000 feats
today I'm a mountain soul today I've braved the
iron & stone, the smoke, the wind
a bell tolls.....

they talk of fables & mountain legend I greet
them & proceed to file into their
small, green & brown thatched homes perhaps a
remnant & extension
of mother earth, a tribute to the glory of nature's
elements

I shake their hands & lower my haversack
bearing gifts from a Mumbai mall in Worli
the one just before Sea Face
that mall that was once a heartbeat
That mall that would seem alien to the tribe

We exchange glares, I play my guitar, sombre &
mellow increasing the tempo
the young pahadi girls dance as I play those old
songs, of forgotten lovers
we eat & drink hearty

a light drizzle cuts the festivities
which now turns into the withering of the clear
sky
like a doorway that has been shut or a
submarine's sonar
in a blind spot, unannounced showers
I can feel the rain as it pierces bolts of ice,
almost pellets
the first shower to mark the onset of harvest
rows of cart trails & bullock cart tracks

Scrawled on walls of the hallowed indestructible
years
those college days of pondering
those chimes & times of youth & recklessness
that did evoke a passage a prominent yet
forgotten time

we gather'd like tribesmen for the sesh
6th floor penthouse apartment
surrogate numbness
fragments of Himalayan recreation

Pink, brown, and crystalized
We lit the pipes, chillums
a juke joint
An afternoon of laughs that faded into a body
high
benumbed and engulfed

Himalayan ice

Two Of A Kind, Be Kind

Do you remember those gigs at Razz?
Nights in the Bombay rock scene
long before the jazz?

The travel there
your father's car
or by cab

Fiat Padmini
Kaali peeli
dragging
itself through
the heaviness of
the city at night

Bombay skyline
sinking into the breach afar

& the bhayanak mosh pit
that you dared me to enter
Smoking cigarettes
w/ the ocean at view

banter
placid food
& just talking to you two

the envy
of the crowd
as I stood there
waiting for
the machine smoke
& strange hoards
to clear
to live those moments
a little more near

the two young girls that crossed my path
the brunette was nobility
the dark haired one, destiny

we made our way to the entrance
of the teenage day-dirt-dream
nights of rock and roll
gigs of the past
before the past took its toll

I stayed awake long into the midnight
we spoke of tunnels to your rooms
of laughs, jokes, alcohol and dunes

Trains from Churchgate station
evenings on the wing
clothes & capers
stories of sports
idiot friends
and foes
hidden in hookah smoke

the drinks were up
in a Sundance routine
just drifting through
lanes and plains
skipping class
walking by the seas
in perpetual disdain

that I would go away
& forget those days
only to come back
& think of them
in times I was astray

those movies
Eros or Regal
on the knife edge of boredom
nice & easy every time

kicking hackey sacks
in catching breaks

to give us cheap thrills
long before the
pain and the pills

A camp in Goa
that drunken adolescence
sitting at the entrance
of the compartment door
that made stained
memories
like spilling the beans
in an online messenger
chatroom

only to burn bridges
like tired rivers
that ran their course
just as good as our word
just as good as our looks

I saw you
drifting hand to hand
The teenage dream was here
for you and me
in the Bombay bandstand

A Lull

You tell me that
the sun can be found
beyond a star
That you would wait
till you heard my guitar
from afar

You tell me that all things must pass
& that a new day is a dawn
where the pain from yesterday
is washed in the waves of today's storm

That a dream of the day is part of a daydream
That all is sacred in the night
& filled with secrets
murmurs & candle light

That each day is a moment
Of a lifetime in life's photo reel
That each moment's value
must not be held
by the day's end
in what we feel

That time is an impasse
& hides behind the ocean

That we always dance close
to the ones we love

That an architect made
buildings but never
lived in them rent free

That I was a sailor
That needed an
anchor in her heart

& that my ship would
move with its beat
even if we were apart

That I was an artist
That needed a muse
who could heal
the pain away
as sure as the sea

That I could resurface
from the depths
just like tomorrow
follows yesterday

That we
hold on
& keep track
of a love
of an absentee

& drift into the lull
straight ahead

Fashion In The 21st Century

The marching rattle
the proficient posers
& camera flashlights

Into the neon night
The swell of the gala
the DJ leaves last
she has to do the dishes
& wake her boy for school
in the morning

the planet is exploding
all the people wander
in a dream
waiting in hope
for a silver cloud
a new golden sun
or a bullet train

the path trails into the mist
the radio station is
floating in the void
faceless
& you can touch the sound
but it's fleeting and

moving away
moving away
moving away
to some other land

the people smile sometimes
but most of the time they don't

the bells ring in the distance
the crowds roar in pauses
the piano doesn't play itself
the ghosts collect on the shelf
stopping for b&w cinema

the technology becomes outdated
the machines shovel shit
& clean the garage & backyard
that the Dow Jones is in millions

the fridge moves around the house
the planets become colonized
the little girl's balloon
is tattooed on the wall
the microchips are barely visible

that the planet is moving towards
something more complex
with every passing century

but the melancholy remains
even in three thousand leagues
under the sun or some new star
and three hundred millennia
where the underwater mountains
became islands & continents
& the need to find love remained

that clothes define style
that style is periodic
that it even matters

I picked up the first t-shirt
& shorts I saw in my cupboard
today

And what do the children
learn in school?
And what's fashion worth anyway?

Yon Lies A Boat Waiting

The silence
The rival dealer
a smile sometimes
holding on to
sad songs
& the fading
echoes of a loneliness
cast into a petrol
fueled firepit

Of thoughts
The wounds that we share
Like a cosmic motion
Of terrace paint
& a shooting star

Birds come & go
But the wolf remains
A heart is never far
to dive into

The tides
& movement
& space

My privateer she calls,
And a boat lies waiting

A Western, A Wedding

A Mexican underdog
A pistolero,
pirata,
guitarslinger
that Latino touch
to his fingerstyle

a desperado
of the quick
& dead
sailed ships
to lands afar
amidst the loot
& bloodshed

lands of prairies
& ranches of
San Cristóbal de las Casas
nights under
a wolf's moon
a bottle
& a wish

wounded nights
on horseback

unforgiving
heat
& endless travel
an outlaw
by design

& the woman that
freed him from
the dungeon
he loved her because
she reminded him of freedom
freedom once taken away
freedom they
took for granted

enterprise
those wild eyes
that gave him peace
& the care & love
that lingered to see

& to catch a glimpse
of the Mexican dream
that satin white
the morning sunlight
the reason he would fight

They danced in the sand
by a beach fire

the ocean
& expanse of blue
breathless to view
just the two

The children frolic
& throw the cake around
the groom is carried
by his best mates
blood brothers
& bandits

The damsel
a woman of substance
who stands strong against
the ill winds

Moments of bliss
that he thought
he would never live

that picture he kept
in the moment he wept

she's beautiful
short black dress
the night is young

she's been a chase
she's been alone

he takes the stage
with his guitar
pays tribute to the guests
& the love for his bride
as the celebration begins
under the starlit skies

the guitar begins to strum
the audience clap in tandem
tonight they will dance into
the dawn

A celebration
a beginning
a journey
of a love beyond

w/ the tunes
echoing through eternity
A Western, a wedding
circa. 1863

Abstract Street Pact

Meandering
a niche sound
ultrasound doppler
camping
underneath
the arching willow
& the evening run

another jazz bar
another daydrift
another short ride
people draped
facelessness

inside out
trudging slow
& calm

pensive in mind
the will to survive
it'll stick around

street corner pub
& grocery store
(the camera pans)
everything you do

everything in blue

Another sun
that sinks
into the shadows

heart on sleeve
floating souls
staring into
the beginnings

of their own ingenuity
& design

a song that welcomes
the night

walking the streets
with sidewalk art
that expresses an idea,
a revolution,
for souls skirting by
the longing dies

traffic signals
search parties
& strobe lights
casting a glimmer,
a cinematic projector

a film tape
a spinning wheel

the entrance is enchanted
by the torn down
desert pit
w/ the scorpion's armour
& a hot hand fallacy

a piercing dance
of a door-to-door salesman
of everyday journeys

a pulse of meaning
watching the progressive
scenes
sink
fade
sink
fade

city light
not too far ahead
or not too far behind

We'll get there
even if it's not
written in
the signs

Kamala

Born in a country
not yet free
in the South of India
April 1943

she bloomed
like the grandest
flower
in independence

with inner strength
and music in her veins
she raised her kin
w/ values & honor
unfettered & unphased

through every bright & dark day
through every storm & sun

now they dance to the tune
of a 5-piece samba
but without her
& her other half
the dance would not be complete

it was our intersection
& the divine will of meeting
a celestial collision
of souls crossing paths
for this short ride
that you were here
you loved us all
& held us dear

You bowled me over in windy Bokaro
You took me to the aeroplane garden
when the star was born
You told me stories of heroes & doing good
You spoke only Tamil but were always
understood
You massaged my wounds
for days on end
w/ love for a grandchild I cannot comprehend

Now the stars will come together
& light your way
as the Gods you prayed to
will adorn your path today

Thank you grandmother
a home for hearts
of all those you touched

the kindest soul
an artist of old music
with a devotion & passion
that we would always discuss

a constant, a shelter
that kept us all together

no cloudy moment
nor storm could stir

A lotus flower
of love & life
you were

Everyday Heroes

We are everyday heroes
suspended in a confluence
receding iron boards
—unplanned— warning
a mellow withholding

Cast amongst lilac
textures & suburban
—sonnets— that envision
the curtain openings

the coasts are dried &
composed in E minor
the spin is around the sun
the particles
—dividing

      but after it caves in,
the shopping cart shapeshifts
the theories have no gravity

Loops of samples:
      a choice of catharsis
      a word from a lady
      a bloodhound that bathes in shapes

the crackle of a 30s vinyl
those strings that cry
a school bell that urges the tides
& the halos that swim
inside the tapestry

Everyday heroes
for the silent battles fought
disappear & march into
the arms of progress

Interludes

Who goes there, down the old NH7? The poison
has been cast
The sour soul train has embarked, but you are
still here
The cokehead & the thief are running amok
The bar stool is bending in a time inversion

The portfolio is sinking, the instruments are
ablaze
A gas mask is needed for the coming of the
surfer's wave
An old Maruti 800 begins splitting like a mosaic
You can take your images of dawn & complex
leaffall

You can lie unperturbed, and draw the Shaolin
master's slogan
You can cancel the parcel to the landslide by the
shoe shop
Are you entangled in the indecision of belief?
Or are you a skateboarder looking to sleep under
a thatched hillock

Are these intertwining dreams the end? Can the
evening pass slow
& —radio static—
                    under the clothes of a vacant
apartment lot
                    looking at a burning chariot
embezzling the sky into descent
                    a spinning record player, a lit
cigarette

Halt! Before you look into my eyes,
Tell me about that pain that robbed you of a
good time
The bulbs here are not electric
the streets are passageways to dragon lairs

—no— The old couple look out the window
And count their breath, in interludes

Indian Buddha

Soundcheck late 2020s
                    the hammer that holds
                    the string to its bow
                    the electric & analog
The show is about to kick into the favourite
groove
                        —extended— in the flood
of people
The Ghost that dawned
the intent that was fleeting

Carousels of letters & artwork
& arrays of changing borderlines
that propels the spirit
white gowns strewn amongst the parapettes:
                        When did the time eclipse
the fragments?
                        Where did the tales languish
in the video game?

The stage is starboard, the sails are bathed in a
Bombay sleeve
The capacitors are cranking up the shoulder to
lean on

The mornings are golden, the afternoons feel
like a frown
                         Where must the battalion
march now?
                         The morse code comes
in.....

The Parvati River begins to assert its occasional
cool
The bridge o'er the river begins to dance to its
passing
—a hiss—

The moon could pierce the howls from the
wolfpack
The air density reveals a DaVinci starmap &
ethereal edit section
The skies combine in dark blue hue
peaks of bliss and strength and wonder

—a crash— the waves on the shoreline drift into
the filters of the decks
The cards that the gambler had remained the
same
Smoke trucks evaporating with the landing at
Dunkirk
A hundred COs and units of a 1000
"You need a song to get by?" the sign read

The edge of history, a world on the peripheries
of the Ads/CFT duality
The ragged thoughts marched on once more

Then
—in quiet contemplation— A comet that blazed
past the sky's perimeters
An inward breath & a release of exhaustion

Hitherto we must find our ground

—peace—amidst the raging war

Indian Buddha